TALKIN' GOLF AND TENNIS

BY JIM GIGLIOTTI • ILLUSTRATED BY JAMES HORVATH

Published by The Child's World®
1980 Lookout Drive • Mankato, MN 56003-1705
800-599-READ • www.childsworld.com

Photo: Cover: Shutterstock: Mr. Suchat (left); Vasyl
Shulga (right). Interior: Newscom: Ray Stub-
blebine/UPI 4B; Hardt/UPI 15T; Eimar Kremser/
Sven Simon 15B. Shutterstock: Gelpi 1L; Olimpix
1R; DaxioProduction 4T; Bama Tanko 6; Kaczor58
7; Andrio 8T; Karamysh 8B; ChenWS 9; Bluekat 10;
Flashon Studio 11; Hannamariah 12; OtmarW 13;
Moinback 14; RTImages 16; Leonard Zhukovsky 17;
Dean Clarke 18; Sinnakorn 20; Igorstevanovic 21

ISBN 9781503835788
LCCN 2019943136

Printed in the United States of America

TABLE OF CONTENTS

INTRODUCTION

"The long hitter pulled the big dog from his bag and let it fly from the tips!" If you don't "talk" golf, that sentence makes no sense. How about this one? "Her forehand volley dropped softly over the net for a winner and a huge break." If you don't talk tennis, you won't know what *that* means. But we're here to help!

Every sport has its own language. The sport's words and phrases mean something to any real fan. The more of those words you can learn, the more you'll enjoy every game you watch. In this book, we'll explore golf and tennis. It's time to grip it and rip it!

▲ *This golfer has "gripped it" and is about to "rip it" from the tee.*

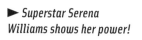

► *Superstar Serena Williams shows her power!*

Every golfer dreams of making an ace. That's a hole-in-one!

Long Histories

Golf and tennis have both been around a long time. Golf started way back in the 1400s. A game like modern tennis began in the 1500s. No one is entirely sure how either sport got its name. The words "golf" and "tennis" come from **Middle English**.

We have aces in tennis, too! They are when one player's serve is not returned by another player.

Majors

The biggest events on the professional golf and tennis calendars are called the "Majors." These are the most important tournaments. They have the most **tradition**. All the best players in the world compete in the Majors. The tennis Majors are the same for men and women. The golf majors are slightly different.

Golf Majors

Men: The Masters, U.S. Open, British Open, PGA Championship

Women: ANA Inspiration, U.S. Women's Open, Women's PGA Championship, The Evian Championship, Women's British Open

GEAR UP

Grab your sticks and head to the course. Or take your strings and get onto the court. Either way, it's time for some outdoor fun! "Sticks" are golf clubs. "Strings" are tennis rackets. That's "rackets," not "racquets"! Rackets are for tennis. Racquets is a fancier way of spelling the word. It's usually used in sports such as badminton or squash.

Golf Clubs

A player is allowed 14 clubs in golf. These are woods, irons, and putters. A good player knows exactly how far and how high she hits every club. Woods make the ball go the farthest. Once made of wood, today they are metal. The putter is used on the "dance floor." That's the green. It's where the cup is. The cup is the hole.

A golf ball is at least 1.68 inches (4.27 cm) in diameter. It goes into a hole that is 4.25 inches (10.8 cm) in diameter.

The Bag

Players keep their clubs and balls in a bag. It has lots of places for tees, markers, and snacks. Tees are small pegs that the ball sits on. They're used for the first shot of a hole only. Markers show where the ball is on the green if one player needs to get out of the way of another. Snacks are important because it can be a long day on the course!

Footwear

Golfers wear shoes with spikes to keep their feet from slipping when they swing. Most spikes are plastic. Tennis players wear, well, tennis shoes. They are made for quick stopping and starting and changing direction. That's exactly what a tennis player does!

The Tennis Ball

A tennis ball is between 2.57 and 2.70 inches (6.5-6.8 cm) in diameter. It is filled with air. Most tennis balls are bright yellow. Why? Because they are easier to see on video and TV screens.

Golf courses come in all shapes and sizes. Golf is always played on grass. Players hit the ball from tee to green, one shot at a time. This diagram shows the names of parts of a golf course.

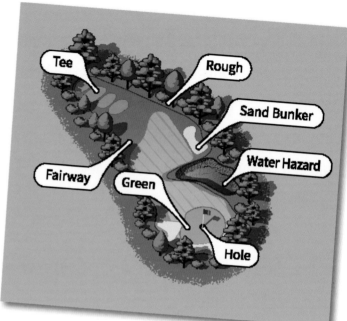

Tee
Rough
Sand Bunker
Water Hazard
Fairway
Green
Hole

Less Is More

In golf, the goal is to get the ball in the hole in as few hits, or strokes, as possible. A golf hole also can mean the entire area from where a player first hits the ball to the cup. A golf course usually has 18 holes. Each hole is measured in yards. Each hole is a par-3, par-4, or par-5. "Par" is the number of strokes a very good player should expect to take on a hole. The longest holes are par-5s.

From Tee to Green

Golfers first hit from the tee box. They aim toward the green. A flagstick on the green shows players where the cup is. A flagstick is . . . a big stick with a flag on top! Except for short holes, a "fairway" leads up to the green. The fairway has shorter grass. It is much easier to hit off than the longer grass on either side of it. That's the "rough." But watch out for the bunkers. They are filled with sand.

◄ Shots from the fairway are usually from level ground.

Not enough time for 18 holes? Check out a shorter "par-3" course. They're fun and take much less time to play!

Golfer Nicknames

Paula "The Pink Panther" Creamer

Ernie "The Big Easy" Els

Brittany "Bam Bam" Lincicome

Jack "The Golden Bear" Nicklaus

Arnold "The King" Palmer

Eldrick "Tiger" Woods

ON THE COURT

Tennis is played on a court. Courts can be outside or inside. Players stand at one end of the court and hit the ball back and forth across the net. The ball has to land inside the lines or else it's "out" and the point is over.

► *Players stand near the net in doubles.*

The Net

The tennis net divides the court in half. It is 3.5 feet (1.07 m) high. Nets are made of nylon **mesh**. Most have a strip of white tape across the top. The strip covers the metal cable that holds the net up. If a serve hits the net, the player serves again. If another shot hits the net and goes over . . . keep playing!

◄ The Tennis Court

A tennis court is 78 feet (23.8 m) long from one end line to the other. The end lines are called the baselines. A ball that hits any line is in play. The court is 36 feet (11 m) wide from one sideline to the other.

► Surfaces

Tennis is played on many different surfaces. The most common are hardcourt, grass, and clay. The Majors are played on a variety of these. The most famous tennis tournament in the world is Wimbledon. It is played on grass. The French Open is on clay. The U.S Open and the Australian Open are on hardcourt.

▲ Alleys

On each side of the court is an "alley." They are 4.5 feet (1.4 m) wide. The alleys are only used for doubles play. Doubles play is when there are two players on each side of the court. When you play singles, keep the ball out of the alley!

PLAYING GOLF

Golf and tennis have funny ways of scoring. Golf counts total number of strokes. But score is often reported against par. Players can be under par, even par, or over par.

▲ *Is she going to drain this putt?*

Golf Scoring

He faced a 10-foot sidewinder, but drained it for a birdie. A "sidewinder" isn't a snake here. It's a **snaking** putt with a big curve to it. Draining a putt means making it into the cup. A birdie is one under par on a hole. An eagle is two under par. One over par on a hole is a "bogey."

Three under par on a hole is called an "albatross." That hardly ever happens!

Putting

Her iron play is awesome. But what really makes her a great player is the flat stick. Irons are numbered from one to nine, plus "wedges" for short shots from around the green and in a bunker. Irons with lower numbers travel farthest. Irons with bigger numbers soar highest. The "flat stick" is the putter. Players must "read," or look carefully, at the green to guess how fast and which way a putt will move.

Obstacles

From the beach, he used a lofted club to get him back onto the short grass. The "beach" is a sand bunker. Sometimes it's called the "cat box." It often takes a wedge with a high **loft** to get over the lip, or raised edge, of the bunker. The short grass is the fairway.

PLAYING TENNIS

Why is a zero score in tennis called "love"? It comes from the French word for "the egg," which is l'oeuf. An egg is shaped like 0.

Tennis doesn't have 1, 2, 3. Instead, tennis calls points in a game 15, 30, and 40. "Love" means zero.

Tie Scores and Ways to Hit

At deuce, she ripped a two-handed, crosscourt backhand to take the advantage. When a tennis game is tied 40–40, it is called "deuce" because a player must win by two points. Crosscourt means hitting the ball diagonally to the opponent's side. A backhand is hit from the opposite side that the player holds the racket. The advantage is to the player who takes a one-point lead at deuce.

Teams

Her perfectly placed volley made it game, set, match for her mixed doubles team. Games and sets make up a tennis match. It takes six games to win a set. It usually takes either two or three sets to win a match. Matches are played between teams of singles, doubles, and mixed doubles. In mixed doubles, each side has one man and one woman.

▼ *Action from a doubles match.*

Tennis Nicknames

Boris "Boom Boom" Becker
Bjorn "Ice" Borg
Mareen "Peanut" Louie-Harper
Martina "The Can't-miss Swiss" Hingis
"Ivan the Terrible" Lendl
Bernard "Tomic the Tank Engine"

Hard and Soft

He answered the overhead smash with a lob that sent his opponent retreating to the backcourt. An overhead is a hit with the racket raised above a player's head. It is always made near the net. A smash is a hard-hit overhead! A lob is a soft shot that arcs high over a player near the net. The backcourt is the area farthest from the net.

GOLF AND TENNIS PEOPLE

Golf and tennis players and officials have some fun nicknames. Here are a few of them.

"Scratch" golfers are the best players. "Duffers" or "hackers" are still trying to get the hang of the game!

Loopers

"Loopers" are caddies. They carry a player's bag around the course. The best caddies can help a player decide which club to use. Long-time loopers are "bag rats" or "lifers." Players who give their caddie a big tip are "princes." Those that don't are "ducks." They duck out of the clubhouse and into the parking lot right after playing!

Weekend Warriors

Only a few golfers are good enough to play for a living. Millions of others around the world work their regular jobs Monday through Friday. Then they play golf on Saturday and Sunday. They are the Weekend Warriors.

The Chair

In pro tennis, line judges on the court call balls in or out of play. They must have good eyes! But the ultimate boss is the umpire. The umpire is called the "chair." That's because he or she sits in a very high chair at center court. Center court is the line where the net is.

At big tennis tournaments, ball girls and ball boys help keep the action moving.

Seeds

"Seeds" are the players that officials think have the best chance of winning a tournament. The No. 1 seed is the top player in a tournament. Seeds are chosen so the best players won't play each other in the early rounds.

GOLF TALK

Want to "talk" golf? Here are a few words or phrases that you need to know.

▲ The big dog just hit a rainmaker. The golfer hopes she doesn't have to yell "Fore!"

Big dog

The nickname for the wood club called the driver. It hits the ball the farthest, but is also the hardest to control.

Cabbage

The rough, which is the longer grass on the sides of the fairway. It's harder to hit the ball out of the cabbage.

Dimples

These are the small **indentations** on a golf ball. They help the ball fly through the air.

"Fore!"

It's what you yell when a ball is going off target and in danger of hitting someone.

Gimmie

For friendly play only! It's a gimmie when a putt is close enough to the hole that your opponent or playing partner counts the next shot as in. You don't have to hit it.

Handicap

A number that all serious golfers work to get as low as possible. It is a way to compare the ability of golfers to each other. The lower the handicap, the better the player.

Sandie

When a player makes par on a hole even after hitting the ball into a bunker.

Snowman

Nobody wants a snowman! It's when a player takes an 8 on a hole. Can you see why?

The tips

The tee area that is farthest from the cup. It's used by the best players.

Up and down

This is when a player looks like she might be in trouble off the green. But she gets her next shot on the green. That's "up." And then she makes the putt. That's "down."

Victory lap

A lap around the course? No way! It's when a putt circles the cup, then drops in. A putt that circles the cup but doesn't drop in "lips out." It might be "afraid of the dark."

Worm burner

A very low shot that barely gets off the ground. It's often a poor shot. But not always. The opposite of a "worm burner" is a "rainmaker." That's a very high shot. It's often a good shot. But not always!

In my sport, a "slice" is a bad thing! It's when a right-handed player hits a shot that makes me curve too far to the right.

TENNIS TALK

In my sport, a "slice" is a good thing! It's a shot that makes me spin both backwards and sideways at the same time. It's a hard shot to hit back.

When you move from the course to the court, you've got more words to know. Here are some key tennis terms.

Break

When the receiving player wins a game against the server.

Dink

This is a low, soft shot hit just over the net.

Fault

This is when a serve is not made in bounds. Two in a row means a "double fault." And that means the opponent wins the point.

Forehand

A hit made from the same side that a player holds the racket.

► The player sets up for a forehand shot.

20

Paint the lines

No, this doesn't mean to get down on your hands and knees with a brush and a can of paint. It means to hit winning shots close or right on to the sideline or the baseline.

Sledgehammer

A winner made by a two-handed backhand shot right down the sideline.

Tiebreaker

A set that is tied in games at 6–6 is decided by a tiebreaker. The first player to get seven points wins. But you have to win by at least two points. So tiebreakers can go on a long time!

Unforced errors

Every player tries to avoid these. It's making mistakes in judgment or action. It's giving away points.

Volley

A ball that is hit back to an opponent before it hits the ground.

Winner

Yes, it's the player who wins a match. But more often, it means any shot that an opponent cannot reach. It scores a point for the shotmaker.

GLOSSARY

diameter (dye-AM-uh-tur) the measure of a straight line through the center of a circle

indentations (in-den-TAY-shuns) notches or dents in a surface

loft (LAWFT) in golf clubs, describes how the head of the club is tilted

mesh (MEHSH) a type of fabric made of crossed material that leaves small holes

Middle English (MID-ul ING-glish) an early form of English spoken from about 1000 to 1500.

snaking (SNAY-king) following a twisting path

tradition (truh-DIH-shun) a way of thinking or doing things passed from one generation to another

IN THE LIBRARY

Cline-Ransome, Lesa. *Game Changers: The Story of Venus and Serena Williams.* New York, NY: Paula Wiseman Books/Simon & Schuster, 2018.

Rockliff, Mara. *Billie Jean! How Tennis Star Billie Jean King Changed Women's Sports.* New York, NY:
G.P. Putnam's Sons Books for Young Readers, 2019.

Webster, Christine. *The Masters.* Calgary, AB: Weigl Publishers, 2019.

ON THE WEB

Visit our Web site for links about golf and tennis:
childsworld.com/links

Note to Parents, Teachers, and Librarians: We routinely verify our Web links to make sure they are safe and active sites. So encourage your readers to check them out!

INDEX

About the Author and Illustrator

Jim Gigliotti is the author of more than 50 books for young readers, including many biographies and lots of sports books! He lives near Los Angeles, CA. James Horvath is an illustrator and cartoonist based in California. He has written and illustrated several children's books, including Dig, Dogs, Dig! and Build, Dogs, Build!